The Generational Style Assessment Response Sheet

Name: ______________________________ **Group/Team:** ________________

This form is provided to score your responses. The resulting information provides insight into your perception of your use of generational styles.

Enter your responses to the 12 scenarios provided on pages 3–5 of the Generational Style Assessment into the grid below by circling the letter that corresponds to your answer (A, B, C, or D) next to the relevant scenario number. Count the number of responses in each column and write the totals in the space provided at the bottom of the grid.

Please make sure that you use sufficient pressure when you fill out this sheet to ensure that your response is transferred to the sheet underneath.

Check your responses by adding the four totals together; you should have a total of 12. If this is not the case, check your responses again to see where you might have made a mistake (such as marking two alternatives instead of just one, for example), and make any necessary adjustments.

SCENARIOS	(1)	(2)	(3)	(4)
1.	B	A	D	C
2.	A	D	B	C
3.	D	C	B	A
4.	D	B	C	A
5.	B	C	A	D
6.	D	B	C	A
7.	B	A	D	C
8.	B	C	A	D
9.	B	C	A	D
10.	D	B	C	A
11.	C	A	D	B
12.	A	C	B	D
Totals				

Once you are satisfied that you have entered your answers correctly, separate the top sheet to show your Generational Style Adaptability score.

Copyright © 2005, Team Publications. All rights reserved.

The Generational Style Adaptability Score

Name: ______________________ **Group/Team:** ______________

This graph will show you which generational styles you tend to use the most. It will also show you the extent to which the influencing or communication styles that you adopt are an effective match to the needs of others from different age groups or generations, providing a wealth of information about your current strengths and development needs.

The scores in the grid below correspond to the response you chose for each scenario. For example, if you choose response C for Scenario 1, the number 2 will be circled in column (iv).

To determine your style adaptability, please add the numbers in each column and write these totals in the sub-total boxes. Finally, add the sub-totals for the four columns together to calculate your Generational Style Adaptability score and write this number in the single box to the right of the graph.

SCENARIOS	(i)	(ii)	(iii)	(iv)
1.	1	3	0	2
2.	3	2	0	1
3.	0	1	2	3
4.	1	0	3	2
5.	2	3	0	1
6.	3	2	0	1
7.	2	0	1	3
8.	1	0	3	2
9.	2	3	0	1
10.	3	0	1	2
11.	2	0	1	3
12.	0	2	3	1
Sub-Totals	+	+	+	=

Generational Style Adaptability Score

Copyright © 2005, Team Publications. All rights reserved.

The Generational Style Assessment (GSA)

Dr. Jon Warner
Anne Sandberg

HRD Press • Amherst • Massachusetts

Copyright © 2005, Team Publications. All rights reserved.

Published by: HRD Press, Inc.
22 Amherst Road
Amherst, MA 01002
(800) 822-2801 (U.S. and Canada)
(413) 253-3488
(413) 253-3490 (Fax)
http://www.hrdpress.com

In association with Team Publications.

All rights reserved. Any reproduction of this material in any media without written permission of the publisher is a violation of international copyright law.

ISBN: 0-87425-849-9

Cover design by Eileen Klockars
Production services by Anctil Virtual Office

Table of Contents

The Generational Style Assessment Introduction 1
Purpose 2
Instructions 2

Interpreting Your Results 7
Determining Style and Style Range 7
Determining Your Style Adaptability Score 8

Understanding the Different Styles 9
The Building Style 9
The Steering Style 9
The Empowering Style 10
The Supporting Style 10

Using the Generational Style Model 12

20s—Spring: The *Dream* Years 13

30s—Summer: the *Productive* Years 14

40s—Autumn: The *Anxious* Years 15

50s—Winter: The *Reflective* Years 16

Summary 17

Generational Style Assessment Model 18

The Four Age Groups/Generations 19

About the Authors 20

References 20

The Generational Style Assessment Introduction

We know that human thinking, decision making, and development are both extremely complex and unique from one person to the next. However, we also accept that there are patterns or styles of thinking and behavior that are readily identifiable. These patterns are associated with differences in inner temperament, nationality, culture, values, gender, and a range of other factors. While none of these, in and of themselves, can fully explain why a person thinks or acts as they do, a particular factor might help to explain some of the reasons, or at least provide a context through which we can make and examine judgments about a person's attitude, behavior, motivation, and beliefs.

A person's age, or the generation to which they belong, is one of many pattern or style factors that help us to better understand a specific individual (or even a whole group of a similar age). In fact, a person's age is a highly influential factor that we all recognize, at least instinctively, when we talk and listen to individuals of an age group different from our own.

This assessment aims to help individuals recognize variations experienced when people from different age groups interact in the workplace, and to raise our awareness of how to adjust or "flex" our own approach to accommodate these variations more effectively. Clearly, our model for looking at the influence of the age factor involves a certain amount of stereotyping of behaviors that are seen to be broadly typical of a particular cohort of people of a certain age. Despite this limitation, as part of a wider approach to look at others from their perspective and not just our own, we believe that this assessment can be helpful by:

- Raising our awareness of the behavioral characteristics most typical for people belonging to each of the four age groups identified in this assessment: 20s, 30s, 40s, and 50s+.
- Identifying through assessment individuals' primary, secondary, and least-used relating styles, including the pros and cons of each with respect to age-related factors and differences.
- Presenting a working model that can be used to "flex," or adapt, one's work style through acquiring new techniques and behaviors that can be used to more effectively relate to and communicate with people from different generational groups.
- Providing a mechanism through which age-related, or generational, differences can be aired and openly discussed as important factors affecting productivity, job satisfaction, management style, and personal motivation.

Purpose

This assessment evaluates the communication or relational style you typically adopt when you are interacting with individuals or groups of people predominantly from one particular age group/generation. For the purpose of this assessment we are using four age groups of people: 20s, 30s, 40s, and 50s+.

The information gathered using *The Generational Style Assessment* provides broad insight into your current style strengths, as well as insight into those areas where some development or enhancement of your communication skills is likely to be helpful in the future. *The Generational Style Assessment* does this by asking you to read a range of different workplace scenarios, and then choose the answer that you feel describes what you would do given the circumstances.

Instructions

- Assume you are involved in each of the following 12 scenarios. Each scenario has four alternative courses of action that you may choose to take.
- Read each scenario and all four alternative courses of action carefully.
- Think about what you **would actually do** in each scenario. Assume that organizational policies are flexible and, for the most part, able to be determined by the manager, unless in direct violation of the law and/or ethical or professional conduct.
- On the Response Sheet, circle the letter which corresponds to the answer you think most closely describes the behavior you would use in the scenario presented.
- Circle only one choice for each scenario.
- Circle a choice for all 12 scenarios. Do not skip any or leave any blank.
- Move through the items relatively quickly.
- Try to stick to your first choice on each item.

REMINDER:

On the Response Sheet, please circle what you think you **would actually do**, not what you think you **should do**. The goal in this assessment is to evaluate what style or behaviors you actually use, not to choose what are considered to be the "right" answers. If there is no alternative course of action that describes what you think you would actually do, circle the alternative that most closely resembles what you think you would do. Please note that this assessment is concerned with matching the most appropriate style in each scenario and not necessarily the best, most effective, or most efficient solution for the individual or the organization as a whole.

In the following scenarios please assume that you are the team leader or mentor to each of the individuals or teams mentioned, and that the possible alternative actions are yours to consider given the circumstances described. Please note that the alternative you select should be based on what you think you **would** do and not on what you think you **should** do.

Scenarios	Alternative Actions
Scenario 1 A team of people, mainly in their 50s, has suggested that they would like to change their working patterns to better cater to the personal needs of individuals within their group.	**You would . . .** **A.** Listen carefully to the suggestions of the individual team members and then leave the group to its own devices, as long as the ideas seem reasonable. **B.** Hold a group meeting to exchange ideas before specifying any particular changes. **C.** Leave the group to its own devices to work these things out for itself. **D.** Inform the group that working patterns are the same for everyone and should not be changed without formal management approval.
Scenario 2 A newly hired individual in his 40s is already getting good work results, but not without irritating a few team members.	**You would . . .** **A.** Hold a brief performance review discussion with the new hire and talk about the issues, in order to agree on how performance could be even better if a more flexible approach were used. **B.** Let the person get on with his job without much interference for the time being. **C.** Get the whole team together socially so that they can get to know the new hire better at a personal level. **D.** Send a short, hand-written note to the new hire telling him that you think he has made a good start, but needs to stop irritating his colleagues.
Scenario 3 An individual in his 30s has shown great reluctance to work as a part of the team, preferring to work on his own as much as possible.	**You would . . .** **A.** Try to find out what makes this individual "tick" and build a better relationship with him. **B.** Spell out that team behavior is expected, but that the individual determines how this is achieved. **C.** Allow the individual to work on his own if productivity is not seriously affected. **D.** Invite the individual to talk about his issues or objections, and try to convince him of the overall need for teamwork.
Scenario 4 Occasionally, a team of people, mainly in their 20s, has been using the company's e-mail system to communicate with each other and with external friends and colleagues on non-work related matters.	**You would . . .** **A.** Talk to each individual personally about the problem, but leave the group to adjust its approach by themselves. **B.** Draw the group's attention to the in-house e-mail policy and ask them to work out a better approach themselves. **C.** Circulate an internal memo informing everyone that non-work related e-mails are considered unacceptable and the practice needs to stop. **D.** Call the group together to discuss and agree what is acceptable and not acceptable in terms of in-house e-mail communication.

Continued ⟶

Scenarios	Alternative Actions
Scenario 5 A valuable female employee in her 50s has been taking a great deal of time off work recently to deal with a terminally ill parent.	**You would . . .** **A.** Talk to the woman and her close colleagues to find out more about her situation, and let her identify what the future is likely to hold in terms of her work. **B.** Spend time with the woman to find out more about the extent of the problem and try to develop a better solution together. **C.** Continue to allow the woman as much time as she needs to sort things out responsibly, given the difficult circumstances. **D.** Specify that the woman's sick time will run out in a certain time frame, and ask her to indicate what she plans to do when this happens.
Scenario 6 A team of people, mainly in their 40s, developed a series of stretching work goals and targets six months ago, but you notice that the whole group is looking tired and jaded and is starting to slip behind.	**You would . . .** **A.** Talk to each individual within the group to try to get some ideas about what they feel may be going wrong. **B.** Write a memo to team members suggesting that targets are slipping, but basically leave them to work things out without any significant intervention. **C.** Call a group meeting to discuss current problems and "brainstorm" a forward path. **D.** Clearly point out to the group that the targets they previously set now need adjusting.
Scenario 7 A newly promoted female supervisor in her 30s is finding some of her older male colleagues difficult to manage and is now letting the situation affect her work.	**You would . . .** **A.** Leave her entirely alone to tackle these inevitable problems. **B.** Tell her that she needs to take no nonsense and show her male colleagues who's boss. **C.** Engage in as much one-to-one coaching as possible to jointly work out what style and approach is likely to work best. **D.** Be available to give her the opportunity to "let off steam," but empower her to decide what to do in the future by herself.
Scenario 8 Two people in their early 20s have been asked to work together to coordinate an internal reorganization of the office. However, many people do not like the "creativity" of the plans and ideas that have been put forward.	**You would . . .** **A.** Having delegated the task, leave the pair alone to do whatever they feel is best. **B.** Write out a list of guidelines that the pair should follow to keep as many people as possible happy. **C.** Ask the pair to talk about whether they think that their plans are likely to suit everyone, and then leave them to decide what changes (if any) are necessary. **D.** Hold a discussion with the pair to try to preserve the best of their ideas, but also indicate some of the needs of others that should also be accommodated.

Continued ⟶

Concluded

Scenarios	Alternative Actions
Scenario 9 A team of people, mainly in their 50s, have been acting as mentors to younger individuals in the organization. This hasn't worked as well as expected in many cases, and a different approach seems necessary.	**You would . . .** **A.** Ask team members to share their mentoring experiences (good and bad) and to come up with a few changes that they believe would help the system operate more effectively. **B.** Gather feedback from mentors and mentees and share it with the team to help shape a new mentoring strategy. **C.** Deliberately leave the group alone to do whatever it feels is necessary. **D.** Minimize any further damage by discontinuing the mentoring program immediately until a better approach can be determined.
Scenario 10 An experienced supervisor in his 40s has been very demanding of his team members and some individuals are starting to feel overworked and under-appreciated.	**You would . . .** **A.** Point out that individual team members seem to be suffering and request that a new less demanding regime be instituted. **B.** Informally chat with the individual to ascertain whether he feels that everything is as it should be, but leave him to sort things out by himself. **C.** Hold a discussion with the individual to see if he might be having any personal or work-related problems or issues. **D.** Work with the individual to jointly determine different possible ways in which goals and objectives can be achieved without de-motivating team members.
Scenario 11 A team of people, mainly in their 30s, have asked whether the organization is prepared to sponsor some charitable work that they would like to do in the local community on the last Friday afternoon of each month.	**You would . . .** **A.** Leave the team to decide whether this proposal meets internal policy and let them continue with their efforts. **B.** Invite the team to discuss with you why their ideas are good for them and the organization as a whole, and agree on the best future strategy to adopt together. **C.** Evaluate the idea on its merits and inform the team of your decision about it (with reasons given). **D.** Ask if you can get involved personally in the charitable work suggested in order to get a better feel for it.
Scenario 12 A woman in her 20s has suggested a social night out for the whole team, and has made reservations for a karaoke bar without asking anyone for their input.	**You would . . .** **A.** Tell her that this isn't the best choice and suggest two alternative venues. **B.** Let the reservation stand and leave team members to choose whether they want to attend or not. **C.** Openly discuss her choice and why she thinks it will be a good social night out for the team. **D.** Chat with the individual about her choice and about who might enjoy and who might not, and identify ways in which this can be made better for all.

Concluded

Interpreting Your Results

Determining Style and Style Range

Your scores on the Response Sheet show the style or styles you tend to adopt most frequently in talking to people in different generations or age groups.

Three important pieces of information come together to form your Generational Style Profile:

1. **Your Primary Style.** Most individuals have a favorite, or primary, relational style. An individual's primary style is one they feel most comfortable with or selected most often. The column on the Response Sheet that has the **greatest number** of responses indicated is your **primary style.**

2. **Your Secondary Style.** Secondary, or supporting, relational style(s) tend to be your "back-up" style(s) when you are not using your primary style. Your **second highest total** on the Response Sheet is/are your **secondary style(s).**

3. **Your Style Range.** Style range refers to the total number of columns on the Response Sheet where you have two or more responses. For ease of reference, you can transfer your column total scores from the Response Sheet to the boxes in the grid below.

Style range provides you with a sense of how flexible you are in varying types of behaviors you engage in when attempting to influence others. Having two or more responses in each of the four quadrants suggests a high degree of flexibility. The greater your style range, the more likely you are to accommodate the needs of different people of all ages/generations, and flex your style or behavior accordingly. However, if your style range is restricted to one or two quadrants, you may find it more difficult to flex your behavior.

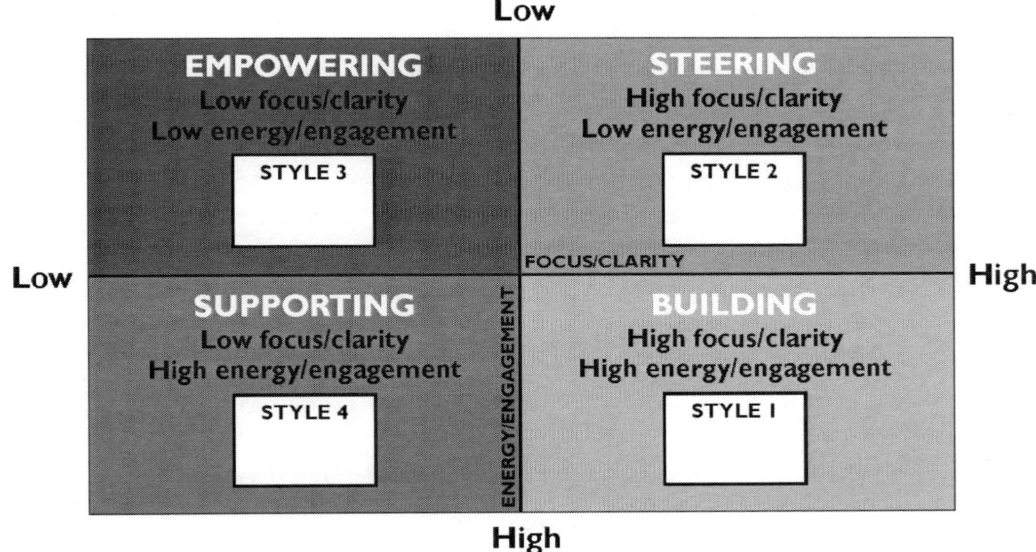

Determining Your Style Adaptability Score

Style adaptability is measured on the second page of *The Generational Style Assessment* Response Sheet.

Style adaptability is the degree to which an individual is able to "flex" their style to match the needs of an individual or team, predominantly from a particular age group/generation. Unlike style range, which shows an individual's degree of "know-how" with different influencing or relational styles, style adaptability measures "know-when": a person's ability to use the appropriate style in the appropriate situation.

On the second page of the Response Sheet, points are given for each alternative action selected for the twelve scenarios provided in the assessment. The number of points awarded is determined by how well the alternative action selected matches the situation. A "3" response indicates the best fit. A "0" response indicates that an action was selected that has a low probability of success.

The use of a point system allows your style adaptability to be expressed as a score. The possible adaptability score ranges from 0 to 36. Expressing adaptability as a score allows some generalizations to be made based on numerical benchmarks:

30–36 Scores in this range indicate an individual with a high degree of adaptability. The person accurately diagnoses the needs of different age groups/generations in different situations, and makes the necessary adjustments in terms of style accordingly.

24–29 Scores in this range reflect a moderate degree of adaptability. This score usually indicates a pronounced primary generational communication style, with less flexibility in secondary styles.

0–23 Adaptability scores of 23 or less indicate a need for self-development to improve both the ability to diagnose generational needs and to use appropriate communication behaviors, and alternative or better-matched styles in different scenarios.

Understanding the Different Styles

The Generational Style Assessment suggests that two underpinning scales, or dimensions, exist in all attempts to communicate with, relate to, and even manage people of different age categories/generations. These scales relate to level of clarity and focus, and level of engagement and energy, of the communicator. Consequently, there are four broad styles based on the various levels of clarity and focus, and engagement and energy, that can be used when dealing with people of different age groups or generations.

- **Building style** (higher levels of energy and engagement; higher levels of clarity and focus)
- **Steering style** (lower levels of energy and engagement; higher levels of clarity and focus)
- **Empowering style** (lower levels of energy and engagement; lower levels of clarity and focus)
- **Supporting style** (higher levels of energy and engagement; lower levels of clarity and focus)

The Building Style

The Building style is often appropriate to use with people in their 20s; this style appears in the lower right corner of the model. The Building style is characterized by an interaction and communication style that is clear and focused, as well as energetic and engaging. This style is highly interactive, typified by give-and-take communication; that is, offering information and asking questions to engage the energy and commitment of the 20-something individual to accomplish the right work goals and objectives. People in this age group are learning and testing what they can do and what they like to do, and often the range of behavior for people in this age group is wide and diverse. Leading someone in his or her 20s requires supportive mechanisms to be in place, and communication skills and strategies that make work expectations crystal clear. This style involves active coaching and direction to build skills and involvement.

The Steering Style

The Steering style is often appropriate to use with people in their 30s; this style appears in the upper right corner of the model. The Steering style is characterized by an interaction and communication style that is clear and focused on the work, but requires lower levels of energy and engagement on the part of the communicator (i.e., manager or person using this style). In this quadrant, it should often be the speaker's, or manager's, intent to "steer" the 30-something person toward the right and most salient goals and objectives. However, it is generally not as necessary to do so with high levels of energy, enthusiasm, and engagement as it is with workers in their 20s. Generally, people in their 30s are settling down or forming a life structure that supports the dreams and values established in their 20s. They have built up a great deal of mastery, skill, and know-how, but are more likely to be wrestling with direction and the central focus of their efforts. It is during this decade that most people, if they have leadership abilities and aspirations, begin to ascend the corporate ladder or pursue a technical specialty or ambition. Quietly "steering" the 30s worker can be much more effective than simply telling him or her precisely what to do; people in this age group look for clear directions but are happy to be given broad frameworks or guidelines, and then be left to accomplish the goal on their own.

The Empowering Style

The Empowering style is often appropriate to use with people in their 40s; this style appears in the upper left corner of the model. The Empowering style is characterized by an interaction and communication style that is less focused on being clear and directive, and requires less energy and engagement than some other groups. People in this age group are often at the peak of their working capacity, having attained a high level of expertise, wisdom, and confidence through decades of work experience and interaction with all types of people. Remember, however, that “low” does not mean “no” for both engagement and clarity; everyone in the workplace needs some level of attention, recognition, and encouragement. However, people in this age group are quite clear about what needs to be done and how to get there, requiring less external stimulus. People in this age group often have “arrived.” They might lack the optimism and passion of those in other age groups at times, but they have come to grips with their own potential and likely career progression. The leader can often let the 40-something worker operate independently and simply be available for his or her questions and individual needs, as these arise.

The Supporting Style

The Supporting style is often the most appropriate style to use with people in their 50s and beyond; this style appears in the lower left corner of the model. The Supporting style is characterized by an interaction and communication style that is enthusiastic and supportive of the individual’s contribution and expertise, and less focused on clarifying performance goals and focusing the individual’s attention on achieving specific goals and targets. People in their 50s and older generally have considerable expertise, knowledge, and skills to offer the work group, and have settled into a role or career that they enjoy and with which they are comfortable. In this respect, people in this age group are generally no longer searching for their best job fit, but might have interests, activities, and goals outside of work that are stimulating and/or demanding. The goal in this quadrant is to keep 50s+ people involved, show them how they are of value to the organization, use their expertise to maximum advantage, and help them manage their affairs so that both work and personal life are fulfilling and achievable. An effective communication technique for this age group is to calmly listen, offer support, and engage the person in collaborative decision making. In this quadrant the individual(s) might be more likely to dominate and control the communication, while the leader is best left to offer general encouragement rather than to suggest specific outcomes or actions. People in this age group are often likely to draw on their experience in terms of direction, but like to feel that they are part of a team in terms of relationships.

In summary, the four generational styles described below are useful for quick reference:

- **High clarity and focus/high energy and engagement behavior (Style 1)** is referred to as "Building," because the communicator attempts to use two-way communication and relationship-based support to get people to psychologically "buy into" issues or decisions. This style is likely to be most effective when talking to or working with individual(s) in their 20s (or an individual of any age who appears to need specific guidelines for future action offered in a warm, energetic, and friendly way).
- **High clarity and focus/low energy and engagement behavior (Style 2)** is referred to as "Steering," because this style is characterized mostly by one-way influence and communication. This style is likely to be most effective when talking to or working with an individual(s) in their 30s (or an individual of any age who appears to need a broad framework for future action).
- **Low energy and engagement/low clarity and focus behavior (Style 3)** is labeled "Empowering," because the style allows individuals or teams to be relatively independent and "run their own show." The communicator mainly delegates, since this individual is usually willing and able to take responsibility for directing his or her own path. This style is likely to be most effective when talking to or working with individual(s) in their 40s (or an individual of any age who appears to need very little in the way of specific guidelines or relationship-based behavior).
- **High energy and engagement/low clarity and focus behavior (Style 4)** is called "Supporting," because the communicator tends to want people to be involved in decision making through two-way or collaborative discussion. This style is likely to be most effective when talking to or working with individual(s) in their 50s+ (or an individual of any age who appears to need a warm and friendly style, but only loose direction or input).

NOTE: It should always be remembered that all four of these generational communication styles offer somewhat stereotypical views of both the style quadrant and the age group/generation to which the style is most often effectively applied. Therefore, this information should be used as one more piece in the successful communication jigsaw puzzle, not in a one-dimensional or slavishly predictive way.

Using the Generational Style Model

> *"Life's racecourse is fixed. Nature has only a single path and that path is run but once, and to each stage of existence has been allotted its appropriate quality."*
>
> —Cicero

Across all cultures and epochs, and all classes and races, the experience of aging is universal for all people in all societies. "From a biological standpoint," observed Chinese philosopher Lin Yutang, "human life almost reads like a poem. It has its own rhythm and beat, its internal cycles of growth and decay."

In order to look at the "cycles" of time or phases in life that make most sense, we have two main options from which to choose. The first of these, and often the most popular, is to look at generational groups according to the year of birth (in roughly 20-year eras). Therefore, it is commonplace to talk of "Builders" or "Traditionals" (born in 1924 to 1943), "Baby Boomers" (born in 1944 to 1963), "Generation X" (born in 1964 to 1983), and finally "Generation Y" or "Nexters" (born in 1984 to 2000). All four of these generational groups are in the workplace today, and each can be characterized as one cohesively behaving group based on the eras in which they grew up or were influenced in their formative years (through social, economic, political, and technological influences).

While this is a useful and interesting way to look at differences between generations, this approach does potentially suffer by rigidly anchoring all people in a large, fixed stereotype according to when they were born. In addition, it assumes that a Baby Boomer, for example, would think in similar ways whether they were 25 or 75.

To overcome these limitations, the second option in considering life phases is to look at the aging process as a cycle through which every individual must travel. Pythagoras was among the first of western thinkers to interpret life as a cycle of four phases for an individual. He suggested that these phases were roughly 20 years long, and further stated that each could be usefully associated with a season: the **Spring** of youth, the **Summer** of early adulthood, the **Autumn** of midlife, and the **Winter** of older age. Many others (Shakespeare, for example) have maintained this analogy and extended the use of the theme ever since. More recently, Gail Sheehy (1976), published the enormously popular pop psychology book, *Passages: Predictable Crises of Adult Life,* which covered the principal challenges and concerns facing individuals passing from one developmental adult life stage to the next.

Using this broad model, we can argue that we connect our life cycle with the seasons of nature not only to link our personal past to our personal future, but also, as Shakespeare might have suggested, to locate our own life within a larger social drama; as Sheehy notes, to grow to one's full potential.

Like the seasons, the four phases of life blend into each other guided by a rhythm that allows some variation. Whereas an actual season's length is determined by the time from solstice to equinox, the length of each life cycle phase is determined by one particular span of time. In *The Generational Style Assessment,* we have described four particular stages or phases of an individual's adult working life; people in their 20s, 30s, 40s, and 50s+. These are seen to be short enough for the stereotype to usefully apply to most people in the age group described (a decade), but also long enough to allow for real differences between generations to be observed.

The four age groups are described in brief on the following pages.

20s—Spring: The *Dream* Years

Young Adult (20s). This is a period of exploration, leaving home, and trying out new possibilities for a career. It is a period of escaping from parental domination, of substituting friends for family, and of defining oneself as an adult and starting to shape an initial life structure. Young adults are often graced with strength, quickness, endurance, and output, the "springs" of youth. People in their 20s can also be reckless and selfish.

During this period, the construct of career maturity is added to exploration, i.e. the idea that there are age-appropriate skills to be mastered at every career stage. It is healthy for people in this age group to keep their options open, explore many alternatives, and avoid pre-maturely committing to one job, employer, or even career. This is the time for young adults to explore their possibilities, test some initial choices, and build a provisional life structure that is both viable in the world and suitable for them as an individual.

The 20s are marked by setting a life direction or forming a dream. It's the time of firming up values and deciding what is important in relation to career, family, and interpersonal relationships. Basically, these young adults are answering the question, "What will I do with the rest of my life?" This vision that is forming will probably govern life for the next 15 to 20 years.

Life in the 20s is often marked with many changes because of the forming dream. This is when many people start their careers and engage in long-term romantic relationships. Many marry, and some start a family and settle into a home. The late 20s, particularly, is often a time when the early 20s dream is re-evaluated. This is an urgent time. Sheehy calls this period the "Trying 20s." There's a desire to start to become settled, make sure the career is coming along, and develop an individual sense of identity in the community and with friends. The person in their late 20s is asking the question: "How well am I progressing in the direction of my dream of the early 20s?"

During the 20s, time is often regarded in a future sense; a lot of life is still to be lived. There is often an overriding sense of optimism and open-mindedness. People are able to put up with limitations because they expect the future to be better. They are "paying their dues" so that the future will be bright and rewarding.

The thinking of the 20s is quite black-and-white. Everything is relatively easy, and most questions have precise answers. Life is very busy, but it hasn't become terribly complex yet. Not until the person has moved into the middle years will he or she begin to wrestle with life's deep and perplexing issues, most of which do not have simple answers, or sometimes appear to have no answers at all.

Although individuals are not a "hostage" to their age group, the best generational communication or relational style for leading people in their 20s is "Building" (high Clarity and Focus; high Energy and Engagement). This style supports the black-and-white, more clear-cut directional view of the world that tends to be held, while providing the higher emotional or relational support that is also needed to build commitment and foster development.

30s—Summer: The *Productive* Years

The 30s is a period of intense and significant personal and work life progression and growth. Young adults in their 20s often experience a series of "trial" jobs before increasingly establishing themselves in a more stable or longer-term career path. This process of establishing oneself is the primary task associated with young adulthood, and once stabilized, consolidation and advancement become the next developmental tasks.

The 30s are a time for establishing one's niche in the workplace, getting on with work, and "taking care of business." In their 30s, most people have settled on their chosen career and might be making adjustments and accommodations, but are often working within a defined structure or framework. During this period, many are motivated to "climb the ladder," getting ahead, and becoming more senior and expert in their field. Mentor relationships can occur in the 30s (or continue from the 20s), but the 30-something is becoming more independent and less open to emulation of an admired role model.

Several important concepts surface during this period of life, including career adaptability and career adjustment. In addition, gender differences become apparent as men and women choose whether or not to follow paths congruent with traditional gender roles, or hit particular obstacles or different views in terms of what is and is not considered to be "acceptable."

The 30s are extremely busy years for most people. Many people in their 30s seem to focus only on career, sometimes almost totally ignoring family life and personal relationships outside of work. On the other hand, they might have a combination of interests; family, marital relationship, and occasionally, perhaps a crisis. For this group, juggling is the primary challenge. It's a busy time for those with families as children are born and begin to grow up and the demands of working and raising a family intensify.

The productivity of the 30s is characterized by action and movement; sometimes by doing everything at once. For many, energy is boundless and opportunities are abundant. For those with leadership aspirations, this is the time for moving up the corporate ladder. For those not particularly interested in climbing the career ladder, it might be a time to take on new interests or projects outside work.

Although individuals are not a "hostage" to their age group, the best generational communication and relational style to use with people in their 30s is "Steering" (higher Clarity and Focus; lower Energy and Engagement). This style tends to work well given the busy lifestyle of those in their 30s; there is often a need to give some broad directional advice to 30-somethings, but then they can be left on their own to work out how things should be done and fit in with everything else that is going on in their lives.

40s—Autumn: The *Anxious* Years

Middle Age (40s). The 40s are often marked by anxiety for many people. People in this age group often ask, "Who am I? What have I accomplished? What am I going to do with the rest of my life?" For many, this is a time of letting go of the impossible dream—understanding that one may never become president of the company (or even senior executive), or financially wealthy.

Their 40s is often a time for people to assess gains, possibly asking if the gains are worth the price. "So I have a house in the suburbs, a boat at the lake, and an influential position. Does it give me the personal satisfaction I thought it would? Maybe I should look at some previously ignored alternatives? What about a simple, more self-sufficient lifestyle in the country? What about not trying to be ambitious?" The 40s are often a time of questioning and re-assessment.

The 40s can be characterized as a period when perceptions become more important than chronology. In other words, how a person feels about his or her life experiences is more significant than a chronological timetable indicating years of life. It is a period marked by stress for some, by constraints for others, and by freedom for still others.

This is a period of life that is often characterized by reappraisal, stress, angst, or the need for more freedom. For men, state of health or career accomplishment may predominate. The reason for this fixation on re-evaluation is based on three factors that occur around this period of time: first, a modest decline in body functioning that may be interpreted as a loss of vigor as well as a reminder of one's mortality; second, an age shift that occurs as younger people regard all older individuals as completely different or even alien; and third, a reflective examination of their youthful dreams. For women, this stressful period can be partially due to the beginning or in anticipation of menopause and children becoming more independent and leaving home. Women in their 40s often rethink their marriage, career, children, themselves, and their beliefs. They ask, "Who am I? What have I accomplished? What am I going to do with the rest of my life?"

This time of rethinking life can be called a midlife transition. For a period of time, a breakdown might occur in the individual's lifestyle and thinking patterns. The person might make some apparently dramatic life changes and be characterized by a desire to completely escape. For some, a search for greater meaning arises, as can spiritual crisis. Author Gail Sheehy calls this time "groping towards authenticity."

Although individuals are not a "hostage" to their age group, the best generational communication or relational style to use with people in their 40s can be "Empowering" (lower Clarity and Focus; lower Energy and Engagement). This style tends to work well for this group given their experience level and mastery of their area of expertise coupled with their strong need to "take charge" of their own life even if it is a different kind of life from the one that has been followed to that point. People in their 40s generally do not need high levels of work support, though they might need support and understanding at times to be able to attend to their obligations outside of work, such as family demands and aging parents.

50s+—Winter: The *Reflective* Years

Late Adulthood (50s+). Workers over 50 no longer fit the old stereotype of declining agility and ability, quietly waiting for retirement. Rather, most are exceedingly healthy, experienced, well-educated, and major contributors to the economy and businesses. Most 50s+ might be moving out of "center stage" at work, but continue to play important roles in the organization. They may have also developed consuming interests outside of work, such as becoming politically active, community oriented, and/or family oriented in contributing to the raising of children/grandchildren.

The 50s and beyond is often a happier time for people, as many develop a "no panic" approach to aging based on greater acceptance and approval of one's self. Many people in their 50s move from competing with others to connecting with others, are able to let go of old rules, and find renewal of purpose that can be inside or outside of work. Many find companionship or a zest for aloneness that is satisfying beyond what they experienced in younger years.

Older workers, particularly in their 60s and beyond, are more likely to take up consulting, seek self-employment, perform community service, and they are more likely to work part time. Older workers' attitudes toward career development activities and mobility relate to such factors as current employment (experience or fear of layoffs), tenure or stage in their careers, need for achievement, and need for growth. In addition, fear of stagnation, marketability perceptions, self-esteem, and job market conditions play a role in job or career decision making. A decision to engage in training or retraining can lead an older worker to identity growth and enhanced self-esteem, which in turn may result in greater commitment to future career development goals.

People in their 50s and beyond tend to reevaluate their life direction and become resigned or refreshed with their outlook and decisions. This means that generally, both men and women will have passed through their midlife re-evaluation and are now using their wisdom and experience to make a significant impact. They have prioritized their lives, thrown away unnecessary obligations, and focused their energies on their redefined dreams.

This reflective age group has a lot to offer younger age groups, because they have a time focus that sees almost all of life. They're well beyond the competitive emphasis of the young adult or early midlife person. They have accumulated life experience and are able to look at life issues with a much more mature perspective.

Although individuals are not a "hostage" to their age group, the best generational communication or relational style to use with people in their 50s+ can be "Supporting" (high Energy and Engagement; lower Clarity and Focus). The Supporting style downplays clarifying targets and setting a strong direction, in deference to offering strong support and encouragement for these employees to share their expertise and wisdom with others. This style tends to work well for this group given the strong need for those at this life stage to continue to feel that they are wanted and valued, and play an important role on the team.

Summary

"Perhaps every generation feels that its life problems are unique in character and severity—and each of them may be right. We shall not know until we learn how to study the adult life course in some depth, and with full appreciation of its complexity."

—Daniel Levison

This assessment has suggested that there are four age groups/generations that exist in the workplace. These are people in their 20s, 30s, 40s and 50s+.

All of these groups can generally be seen to engage in collective behavior that is (to some extent, at least) governed by their age or overall level of maturity. To illustrate this we have used the seasonal analogy of spring, summer, autumn, and winter.

Although we have included more extensive information, a brief synopsis of the four age groups used in this assessment is shown on the next page. This also shows the four generational relating or influencing styles likely to be most effective in relation to each age group that can be employed by an individual. The four styles (Building, Steering, Empowering, and Supporting) arise from intersecting two dimensions; the level of clarity and focus required by an individual or group, and the level of energy or engagement that is needed.

In this assessment, we have given individuals a wide range of information about their communication style and how they might increase their flexibility when it comes to relating to all age groups or generations. This includes an individual's:

1. **Primary and secondary generational relating style**
2. **Style range** (or ability to "flex" their behavior when required to do so)
3. **Style adaptability** (or how well they can accommodate people from different age groups in their thinking and action)

Having gained this insight, individuals may use the model on the next page to help them improve their generational style flexibility in the future. This means using all four styles when it is appropriate to do so and becoming more conscious of generational factors when seeking to communicate with, or manage, individuals or groups.

NOTE: The model includes a box in each quadrant of the chart to record assessment scores from the first page of the Response Sheet. It also includes four additional boxes at each corner of the model. These can be used to write in the percentage mix of ages in a specific team or group of people, thus affording the opportunity to adopt a style that is likely to be best suited to the majority of people.

Generational Style Assessment Model

The Generational Style Assessment has four style types, shown in the model below. Simply determine which age group you are dealing with or calculate the percentage balance of ages in group situations and "flex" your style to best meet the needs of the majority of team members.

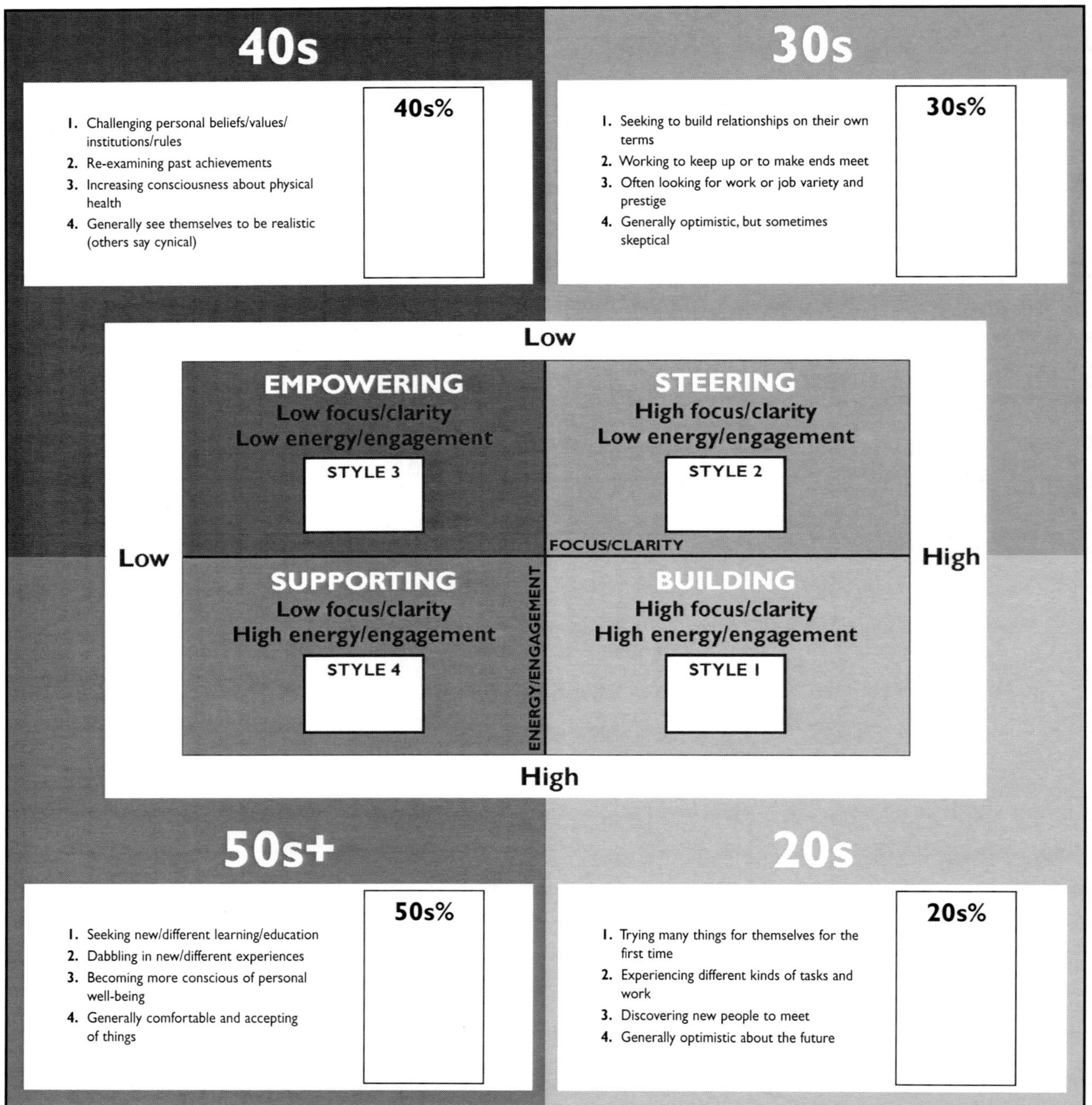

The Four Age Groups/Generations

40s (AUTUMN)	30s (SUMMER)
(Often called the Baby Boomer Generation)  **Building, Education, Reflection**	*(Often called the Gen X Generation)*  **Consolidation, Establishment, Focus**
50s (WINTER) *(Often called the Builder Generation)*  **Acceptance, Enlightenment, Wisdom**	**20s (SPRING)** *(Often called the Gen Y or Nexter Generation)*  **Discovery, Enthusiasm, Exploration**

About the Authors

Dr. Jon Warner, CEO of the Worldwide Centre for Organisational Development in Australia, has 25 years experience with a number of major multi-national companies in the United Kingdom, Europe, the United States, and Australia. This experience has included time as a senior staff manager in human resources and a number of line roles with responsibility for large groups of people. During the past 10 years, Jon has been involved in broad-ranging organizational consultancy and the pursuit of best practice leadership. This consulting has taken him into a number of major organizations such as General Motors, Mobil Oil, the National Bank, Duke Energy, BTR, Qantas, HSBC, United Energy, Air Products and Chemicals, and Dow Corning. Jon is also a widely published author, having written or co-authored more than 40 books and 20 assessment instruments.

Anne Sandberg owns and operates Predict Success®, a leading California-based organizational consulting firm. Predict Success specializes in employee and management assessments, organizational surveys, job analysis, 360-degree feedback process and delivery, HR program design, competency modeling, and corporate training. Predict Success's clients include Fortune 500 companies, and public sector entities, as well as start-up businesses. Prior to co-founding the firm, Sandberg worked within the human resources field for over 20 years, both as an independent consultant and in Fortune 500 companies and the public sector. She has a MS degree in Industrial/Organizational Psychology and frequently speaks at industry events. Sandberg is the published author of *Interview for Success* (HRD Press), and *Interview Generator* CD-Rom and online instruments, and has conducted training and certification programs for HR professionals in the United States, Asia and Latin America.

References

The following books might prove to be useful for those people who want to read more about the characteristics and style of different age groups or generations:

1. *When Generations Collide: Who They Are. Why They Clash. How to Solve the Generational Puzzle at Work.* Lynne C. Lancaster and David Stillman. 2002, Harper Business.
2. *Managing the Generation Mix: From Collision to Collaboration.* Carolyn Martin and Bruce Tulgan. 2002, HRD Press.
3. *Boomers, Xers, and Other Strangers: Understanding the Generational Differences That Divide Us.* Kathy and Rick Hicks. 2001.
4. *Generations at Work: Managing the Clash of Veterans, Boomers, Xers, and Nexters in Your Workplace.* Ron Zemke, Claire Raines, and Bob Filpczak. 2000, AMACOM.
5. *New Passages.* Gail Sheehy. 1995, G. Merritt Corp.
6. *Passages: Predictable Crises of Adult Life.* Gail Sheehy. 1976, E.P. Dutton.
7. *Bridging the Boomer Xer Gap: Creating Authentic Teams for High Performance at Work.* Hank Karp, Connie Fuller, Danilo Sirias. 2002, Davies Black.
8. *Beyond Generation X.* Claire Raines. 1997, Crisp Publications.
9. *The Seasons of a Man's Life.* Daniel J. Levison and Alfred A. Knopf. 1978.